'Your idea of fidelity is not having more than one man in the bed at the same time.'

Dirk Bogarde on Julie Christie in *Darling*

Wisecracks
From The Movies

Compiled by
Derek Wyatt

Futura

To: Devon, Erik and Mark

A Futura Book

Copyright © Derek Wyatt, 1987

First published in 1987 by
Futura Publications, a Division of
Macdonald & Co (Publishers) Ltd
London & Sydney

ISBN 0 7088 3078 1

Typeset by Leaper & Gard Ltd., Bristol, England
Printed and bound in Great Britain by
Hazell, Watson & Viney Ltd.,
Aylesbury, Bucks.

Futura Publications
A Division of
Macdonald & Co (Publishers) Ltd
Greater London House
Hampstead Road
London NW1 7QX
A BPCC plc Company

When I write I keep Tolstoy around because I want great limits. I want big thinking.

Mel Brooks

☆

You call this a party? The beer is warm, the women are cold, and I'm hot under the collar. In fact, a more poisonous little barbecue I've never attended.

Groucho Marx in *Monkey Business*

☆

Oh, I realize it's a penny here and a penny there, but look at me. I've worked myself up from nothing to a state of extreme poverty.

Groucho Marx in *Monkey Business*

Jail is no place for a young fellow. There's no advancement.

Groucho Marx in *The Cocoanuts*

☆

One morning I shot an elephant in my pyjamas. How he got in my pyjamas, I don't know.

Groucho Marx in *Animal Crackers*

☆

Take off your clothes, come in, and tell me all about it.

Claudette Colbert in *The Sign of the Cross*

☆

What happened at the office? Well, I shot Mr Brady in the head, made violent love to Miss Morris, and set fire to 300,000 copies of *Little Women*. That's what happened at the office.

Tom Ewell in *The Seven Year Itch*

And now will you all leave quietly, or must I ask Miss Cutler to pass among you with a baseball bat?

Monty Woolley in *The Man Who Came to Dinner*

☆

Fasten your seatbelts. It's going to be a bumpy night.

Bette Davis in *All About Eve*

☆

It's a nice building. You get a — a better class of cockroaches.

James Earl Jones in *Claudine*

☆

Remember me? I'm the fellow you slept on last night.

Clark Gable to Claudette Colbert in
It Happened One Night

I hate cold showers. They stimulate me, then I don't know what to do.

> Oscar Levant in *Humoresque*

☆

How did you get into that dress — with a spray gun?

> Bob Hope to Dorothy Lamour in *Road to Rio*

☆

Insanity runs in my family. It practically gallops.

> Cary Grant in *Arsenic and Old Lace*

☆

Give me a girl of an impressionable age, and she is mine for life.

> Maggie Smith in *The Prime of Miss Jean Brodie*

Waiter, will you serve the nuts — I mean, would you serve the guests the nuts?

> Myrna Loy in *The Thin Man*

☆

You know me. I'm just like you. It's two in the morning, and I don't know nobody.

> Robert Redford in *The Sting*

☆

I don't want to live in a city where the only cultural advantage is that you can make a right turn on a right light.

> Woody Allen on Los Angeles in *Annie Hall*

☆

When it comes to dying for your country, it's better not to die at all.

> Lew Ayres in *All Quiet on the Western Front*

I was thrown out of N.Y.U. my freshman year for cheating on my metaphysics final, you know. I looked into the soul of the boy sitting next to me.

Woody Allen in *Annie Hall*

☆

Boss, life is trouble. Only death is not. To be alive is to undo your belt and look for trouble.

Anthony Quinn in *Zorba the Greek*

☆

I was suicidal, as a matter of fact, and would have killed myself, but I was in analysis with a strict Freudian, and if you kill yourself they make you pay for the sessions you miss.

Woody Allen in *Annie Hall*

☆

Killing is an excellent way of dealing with a hostility problem.

James Coburn in *The President's Analyst*

I can't get with any religion that advertises in
Popular Mechanics.

Woody Allen in *Annie Hall*

☆

The bottom's full of nice people; only cream
and bastards rise.

Paul Newman in *Harper*

☆

In the twentieth century, the main product
of all human endeavour is waste.

Orson Welles in *I'll Never Forget Whatshisname*

☆

I always get the fuzzy end of the lollipop.

Marilyn Monroe in *Some Like It Hot*

Why, you're one of the most beautiful women I've ever seen, and that's not saying much for you.

> Groucho Marx to Margaret Dumont in
> *Animal Crackers*

☆

Oh, why can't we break away from all this, just you and I and lodge with my fleas in the hill? I mean, flee to my lodge in the hills.

> Groucho Marx to Thelma Todd in
> *Monkey Business*

☆

I could dance with you until the cows come home. On second thoughts, I'd rather dance with the cows until you come home.

> Groucho Marx to Raquel Torres in *Duck Soup*

— Oh, I — I'm not myself tonight. I don't know who I am.
— One false move and I'm yours.

Groucho Marx to Margaret Dumont in
The Cocoanuts

☆

Those ain't lies. Those are campaign promises. They expect 'em.

William Demarest in *Hail the Conquering Hero*

☆

— Too many girls follow the line of least resistance.
— Yeah, but a good line is hard to resist.

Helen Jerome Eddy and Mae West in
Klondike Annie

☆

— Goodness what beautiful diamonds!
— Goodness had nothing to do with it, dearie.

Mae West replies to the cloakroom girl in
Night After Night

Well, it's not the men in your life that count.
It's the life in your men.

Mae West in *I'm No Angel*

☆

Why don't you come up sometime and see
me?

Mae West to Cary Grant in *She Done Him Wrong*

☆

You know, there are three things that we
could do right now: you could call a taxi and
go home, or we could go on walking and I
could lecture you on the real dilemma of
modern art, or we could go to my place and
we could thoroughly enjoy each other.

Alan Bates to Jill Clayburgh in
An Unmarried Women

☆

I used to — used to make obscene phone
calls to her — collect — and she used to
accept the charges all the time.

Woody Allen in *Take the Money and Run*

Even when I was making love to you, I had the feeling that you were wondering what time it was.

Robert Montgomery to Bette Davis in *June Bride*

☆

You don't know what love means. To you, it's just another four letter word.

Paul Newman to Burl Ives in
Cat on a Hot Tin Roof

☆

I remember every detail: The Germans wore grey. You wore blue.

Humphrey Bogart to Ingrid Bergman in
Casablanca

☆

I don't want to be worshipped, I want to be loved.

Grace Kelly to John Lund in *High Society*

Love means never having to say you're sorry.

Ryan O'Neal in *Love Story*

☆

As an actor, no one could touch him. As a human being, no one wanted to ...

Walter Matthau in *The Sunshine Boys*

☆

Susan's growing pains are rapidly becoming a major disease.

Myrna Loy in *The Bachelor And The Bobby-Soxer*

☆

I want to be alone.

Greta Garbo in *Grand Hotel*

☆

Go to bed, little father. We want to be alone.

Greta Garbo in *Ninotchka*

I don't want to die alone.

> Richard Todd in *The Hasty Heart*

☆

If there's anything worse than a woman
living alone, it's a woman saying she likes it.

> Thelma Ritter in *Pillow Talk*

☆

I know it's considered noble to accept
apologies, but I'm afraid I'm not the noble
type.

> Joan Crawford in *Female on the Beach*

☆

I'm not a man that people overlook.

> Clifton Wess in *The Razor's Edge*

Available? You're like an old coat that's hanging in his closet. Every time he reaches in, there you are.

Joan Blondell to Katherine Hepburn in *Desk Set*

☆

Oh, my girl! Someone's been sleeping in my dress.

Beatrice Arthur in *Mame*

☆

— What time is it?
— It's the right time, honey.

Dorothy McGuire to Robert Preston in
The Dark at the Top of the Stairs

☆

A week? Are you kidding? This play has got to close on page four.

Zero Mostel in *The Producers*

Martha, will you show her where we keep the, er, euphemism?

Richard Burton to Elizabeth Taylor in
Who's Afraid of Virginia Woolf?

☆

I say, marriage with Max is not exactly a bed of roses, is it?

George Sanders in *Rebecca*

☆

I believe there are two things necessary to salvation. Money and gunpowder ...

Robert Morley in *Major Barbara*

☆

I *am* big. It's the *pictures* that got small.

Gloria Swanson in *Sunset Boulevard*

He's very progressive. He has all sorts of ideas about artificial insemination and all that sort of thing. He breeds all over the world.

Debbie Reynolds in *The Pleasure of his Company*

☆

Men are usually so bored with virgins. I'm so glad you're not.

Maggie McNamara in *The Moon is Blue*

☆

Doesn't scare me a bit. Tough sergeants just roll off my knife.

Martin Milner in *Sands of Iwo Jima*

☆

— Don't big empty houses scare you?
— Not me. I used to be in vaudeville.

Nydia Westman and Bob Hope in
The Cat and the Canary

Good heavens, Agnes! You have a bust.
Where you been hiding it all these years?

> Lucille Ball in *Mame*

☆

— Are you a man of good character where
women are concerned?
— Have you ever known a man of good
character where women are concerned?

Scott Sutherland and Leslie Howard in *Pygmalion*

☆

I can afford a blemish on my character but
not on my clothes.

> Vincent Price in *Laura*

☆

Am I a king or a breeding bull?

> Charles Laughton in
> *The Private Life of Henry VIII*

Christine; I've reached that realistic age when I have to choose between having fun and a heart attack.

Joseph Cotten to Jacqueline Bisset in
The Grasshopper

☆

The prettiest sight in this fine pretty world is the privileged class enjoying its privileges.

James Stewart in *The Philadelphia Story*

☆

How long does it take to tell a woman, 'My wife's come back?' I can say it in two seconds. 'My wife's come back.' You've had two days.

Irene Dunne to Cary Grant in *My Favourite Wife*

☆

With a binding like you've got, people are going to want to know what's in the book.

Gene Kelly to Leslie Caron in
An American in Paris

What do you get in place of a conscience?
Don't answer. I know: a lawyer.

Kirk Douglas in *Dectective Story*

☆

Anyone who wants to get out of combat isn't
really crazy, so I can't ground him.

Jack Gilford in *Catch 22*

☆

They tell me he was so crooked that when he
died they had to *screw* him into the ground.

Bob Hope in *The Cat and the Canary*

☆

People who hate the light usually hate the
truth.

Burt Lancaster in *Separate Tables*

Forty-two percent of all liberals are queer. That's a fact. The Wallace people took a poll.

Peter Boyle in *Joe*

☆

I always say a kiss on the hand might feel very good, but a diamond tiara lasts forever.

Marilyn Monroe in *Gentleman Prefer Blondes*

☆

Don't think too hard Robert. You might hurt yourself.

Victor Moore in *Make Way for Tomorrow*

☆

That's quite a dress you almost have on.

Gene Kelly to Nina Foch in *An American in Paris.*

The only thing you don't do in your dressing room is dress.

Michael Caine to Maggie Smith in
California Suite

☆

Well, there are some people that rarely touch it (drink), but it touches them often.

Marlon Brando in *A Streetcar Named Desire*

☆

I always start around noon — in case it gets dark early.

Peggy Lee's drinking habits in *Pete Kelly's Blues*

☆

I only take a drop when I have a cold. Of course, that cold has been hanging on for years.

Frank Morgan in *Summer Holiday*

— Could you be persuaded to have a drink dear?
— Well, maybe just a tiny triple.

> Lucille Ball to Beatrice Arthur in *Mame*

☆

Mr Brady, it's the duty of a newspaper to comfort the afflicted and to flick the comfortable.

> Gene Kelly in *Inherit the Wind*

☆

It is a far, far better thing I do than I have ever done. It is a far, far better rest I go to than I have ever known.

> Ronald Coleman's last lines in
> *A Tale of Two Cities*

☆

Cancel my appointments.

> Sylvia Sidney's obituary in
> *Summer Wishes, Winter Dreams*

Oh no: it wasn't the airplanes. It was beauty killed the beast.

Robert Armstrong in *King Kong*

☆

He used to be a big shot.

Gladys George on James Cagney in
The Roaring Twenties

☆

Life with Mary was like being in a phone booth with an open umbrella. No matter which way you turned, you get it in the eye.

Barry Nelson on Debbie Reynolds in *Mary, Mary*

☆

She's got those eyes that run up and down men like a searchlight.

Dennie More in *The Women*

It's not a pretty face, I grant you, but underneath its fussy exterior is an enormous lack of character.

> Oscar Levant in *An American in Paris*

☆

I get goose pimples. Even my goose pimples have goose pimples.

> Bob Hope in *The Cat and the Canary*

☆

You know, you never really feel somebody suffering. You only feel their death.

> Art Carney in *Harry and Tonto*

☆

I liked you 'cause I thought you had some feeling, but when you didn't, I liked you even more.

> Mae West in *Go West, Young Man*

Your idea of fidelity is not having more than one man in the bed at the same time.

>Dirk Bogarde on Julie Christie in *Darling*

☆

I'm going to fire some of these people. Gimme the fire bell.

>Groucho Marx in *The Cocoanuts*

☆

Flattery'll get you anywhere.

>Jane Russell in *Gentlemen Prefer Blondes*

☆

She tried to sit on my lap while I was standing up.

>Humphrey Bogart in *The Big Sleep*

Louis, I think this is the beginning of a beautiful friendship.

>Humphrey Bogart in *Casablanca*

— I do not make friends freely.
— You don't make friends, period.

Ronald Reagan responding to Richard Todd in
The Hasty Heart

☆

We were just playing a game called
Photography. You turn off the lights and see
what develops.

Barry Coe in *Peyton Place*

☆

Dear Petronius, you must forgive me if I
seem to have slighted you greatly, but I've
been steeped in my own genius.

Peter Ustinov in *Quo Vadis*

☆

Well, I'll tell you the truth now. I ain't a real
cowboy but I am one helluvah stud.

Jon Voight in *Midnight Cowboy*

A golf course is nothing but a poolroom moved outdoors.

Barry Fitzgerald in *Going My Way*

☆

In College, I majored in geology and anthropology and running out of gas on Bunker Hill. What's your name honey.

Bob Hope to Jane Russell in *Son of Paleface*

☆

Out here, due process is a bullet.

John Wayne in *The Green Berets*

☆

I've had hangovers before, but this time even my hair hurts.

Rock Hudson in *Pillow Talk*

☆

I hope all your teeth have cavities, and don't forget: abscess makes the heart grow fonder.

Groucho Marx in *The Cocoanuts*

It's lavish but I call it home.

Clifton Wess in *Laura*

☆

There's no such thing as total honesty. Not with men. They're all wrapped up in sexual ego.

Kelly Bishop in *An Unmarried Woman*

☆

There may be honour among thieves, but there's none in politicians.

Peter O'Toole in *Lawrence of Arabia*

☆

You know, when it's hot like this — you know what I do? I keep my undies in the icebox.

Marilyn Monroe in *The Seven Year Itch*

Everything was his idea, except my leaving him.

> Dorothy Comingore in *Citizen Kane*

☆

Confess it: you've been hermetically sealed most of your life.

> George Brent in *My Reputation*

☆

Your best, Mr Keith, is only a maximum of inefficiency.

> Humphrey Bogart in *The Caine Mutiny*

☆

You're not a detective — you're a slot machine — you'd slit your own throat for six bits plus tax.

> Don Douglas in *Murder, My Sweet*

I don't mind a parasite. I object to a cut-rate one.

Humphry Bogart in *Casablanca*

☆

You husband has a great deal to be modest about.

Clifton Wess in *Sitting Pretty*

☆

I apologize for the intelligence of my remarks, Sir Thomas. I had forgotten that you are a Member of Parliament.

George Sanders in *The Picture of Dorian Gray*

☆

I don't know why I should act so experienced. It was only my second kiss this year.

Diane Varsi in *Peyton Place*

To hardly know him is to know him well.

> Cary Grant in *The Philadelphia Story*

☆

Laugh now, Heathcliff. There's no laughter in hell.

> Hugh Williams in *Wuthering Heights*

☆

Where's the rest of me?

Ronald Reagan on finding his legs amputated in *Kings Row*

☆

The only people who make love all the time are liars.

> Louis Jordan in *Gigi*

☆

There is no sincerity like a woman telling a lie.

> Cecil Parker in *Indiscreet*

He's saying that life is bullshit, and it is, so what are you screaming about?

William Holden in Network

☆

I don't have a lifestyle. I have a life.

Jane Fonda in California Suite

☆

You're just walkin' around to save funeral expenses.

Valerie Perrine in The Electric Horseman

☆

I do not like to be interrupted in the middle of an insult.

Charles Laughton in The Paradine Case

☆

Maybe love is like luck. You have to go all the way to find it.

Robert Mitchum in Out of the Past

— Mark, you ever been in love?
— No. I been a bartender all my life.

> Henry Fonda and J. Farrell MacDonald in
> *My Darling Clementine*

☆

— You ever been in love, Hoonbeck?
— Only with the sound of my own words,
thank God.

Spencer Tracy and Gene Kelly in *Inherit the Wind*

☆

Just say you love me. You don't have to
mean it.

> Carolyn Jones in *The Bachelor Party*

☆

We have not missed, you and I — we have
not missed that many-splendored thing.

> William Holden in
> *Love is a Many-splendored Thing*

— My ancestors came over on the
Mayflower.
— You're lucky. Now they have
immigration laws.

Mae West putting one on Almira Sessions in
The Heat's On

☆

Women should not think at all. They are not
equal to it.

Robert Bice in *Dragon Seed*

☆

Women should be kept illiterate and clean,
like canaries.

Roscoe Karns in *Woman of the Year*

☆

Dear Poppaea, one woman should never
fudge another. She hasn't the glands for it.

Peter Ustinov in *Quo Vadis*

Women represent the triumph of matter over mind just as men represent the triumph of the mind over morals.

> George Sanders in *The Picture of Dorian Gray*

☆

Certain women should be struck regularly, like gongs.

> Robert Montgomery in *Private Lives*

☆

Chivalry is not only dead, it's decomposed.

> Rudy Vallee in *The Palm Beach Story*

☆

Marriage is like a dull meal, with the dessert at the beginning.

> José Ferrer in *Moulin Rouge*

Getting married is serious business. It's kinda formal, like funerals or playing stuff poker.

William Gargan in *They Knew What They Wanted*

☆

It is a deadly cancer in the body politic, and I will have it out.

Robert Shaw in *A Man for All Seasons*

☆

Make him feel important. If you do that, you'll have a happy and wonderful marriage — like two out of every ten couples.

Mildred Natwick's advice to Jane Fonda about Robert Redford in *Barefoot in the Park*

☆

Marriage is not forbidden to us, but, instead of getting married at once, it sometimes happens we get married at last.

Isabel Jeans in *Gigi*

It's cyanide cut with carbolic acid to give it a mellow flavour.

Robert Ryan in *The Iceman Cometh*

☆

She is playing solitaire with her memories.

Marita Hunt in *Anastasia*

☆

They can't censor our memories, can they?

Felix Bressart in *Ninotchka*

☆

There are no great men, buster. There are only men.

Elaine Stewart in *The Bad and the Beautiful*

☆

Men don't get smarter when they grow older. They just lose their hair.

Claudette Colbert in *The Palm Beach Story*

Jack, there's something on everybody. Man is conceived in sin and born in corruption.

Broderick Crawford in *All the King's Men*

☆

A man should be what he can do.

Montgomery Clift in *From Here to Eternity*

☆

A man ought to do what he thinks is right.

John Wayne in *Hondo*

☆

— It is written that there are only two perfectly good men — one dead, the other unborn.
— Which are you?

Mae West responding to Harold Huber in *Klondike Annie*

She tries to read my mind, and, if she can't
read my mind, she reads my mail.

> Walter Slezak talking of Ginger Rogers in
> *Once Upon a Honeymoon*

☆

Boston's not just a city. It's a state of mind.
You can't move away from a state of mind.

> Ronald Colman in *The Late George Apley*

☆

Huw is a scholar. Why take brains down a
coal mine?

> Donald Crisp in *How Green Was My Valley*

☆

If you don't mind my mentioning it, Father,
I think you have a mind like a swamp.

> Diana Lynn in *The Miracle of Morgan's Creek*

What is there for you to say? We both know that the mind of a woman in love is operating on the lowest level of the intellect.

Michael Chekhov in Spellbound

☆

Oh, Jo, why can't you learn from my mistakes? It takes half your lifetime to learn from your own.

Dora Bryan in A Taste of Honey

☆

You can be young without money, but you can't be old without it.

Elizabeth Taylor in Cat on a Hot Tin Roof

☆

— Money isn't all, you know, Jett.
— Not when you got it.

James Dean responding to Elizabeth Taylor in Giant

We had some money put aside for a rainy day, but we didn't know it was going to get this wet.

Jane Connell in *Mame*

☆

Sentiment has no cash value.

John Baer in *We're No Angels*

☆

A boy's best friend is his mother.

Anthony Perkins in *Psycho*

☆

You must have been born with that name. You couldn't have made it up.

James Mason in *A Star is Born*

☆

Heh, don't knock masturbation. It's sex with someone I love.

Woody Allen in *Annie Hall*

Not interested in yourself? You're fascinated, Red. You're far and away your favourite person in the world.

Cary Grant in *The Philadelphia Story*

☆

Never trust or love anyone so much you can't betray him.

Montagu Love in *The Prince and the Pauper*

☆

Don't forget the old proverb, Doctor: never trust a man who doesn't drink.

Barry Fitzgerald in *And Then There Were None*

☆

You never pushed a noun against a verb except to blow up something.

Spencer Tracey in *Inherit The Wind*

I don't know how to run a newspaper, Mr Thatcher. I just try everything I can think of.

Orson Welles in *Citizen Kane*

☆

You know the first thing I found out? Bad news sells best because good news is no news.

Kirk Douglas in *The Big Carnival*

☆

She cut off her nipples with garden shears. You call that normal?

Elizabeth Taylor in *Reflections in a Golden Eye*

☆

I'm not being precocious. I'm just a normal fifteen-year-old girl. Actually, I'm not normal. I'm still a virgin.

Lisa Lucas in *An Unmarried Woman*

They're not going to torture me. It hurts.

Bob Hope in *Road to Bali*

☆

Frankly, my dear, I don't give a damn.

Clark Gable in *Gone With the Wind*

☆

I can feel the hot blood pounding through your varicose veins.

Jimmy Durante in *The Man Who Came to Dinner*

☆

The past is a foreign country. They do things differently there.

Michael Redgrave in *The Go-Between*

☆

I'll think about it tomorrow.

Vivien Leigh in *Gone With The Wind*

So, what's the story?

> Richard Castellano in *Lovers and Other Strangers*

☆

I haven't the foggiest.

> Alec Guinness in *The Bridge on the River Kwai*

☆

Whaddaya hear? Whaddaya say?

> James Cagney in *Angels with Dirty Faces*

☆

I was once so poor I didn't know where my next husband was coming from.

> Mae West in *She Done Him Wrong*

☆

He just swallowed his pride. It'll take him a moment or two to digest it.

> Patricia Neal in *The Hasty Heart*

Life without a room to oneself is a barbarity.

Edith Evans in *The Chalk Garden*

☆

The girls call me Pilgrim because every time I dance with one I make a little progress.

Bob Hope in *The Ghost Breakers*

☆

Not Anytime Annie! Say, how could I forget her? She only said 'no' once — and then she couldn't hear the question.

George E. Stone on Ginger Rogers in *42nd Street*

☆

Marry me and I'll never look at another horse.

Groucho Marx in *A Day at the Races*

All of which doesn't answer my question.
Will you marry me? I'm aging visibly.

Raymond Massey in *Possessed*

☆

It's a good night to be abroad and looking
for some.

Albert Finney in *Tom Jones*

☆

How about coming up to my place for a spot
of heavy breathing.

Walter Matthau in *Pete 'n' Tillie*

☆

Why don't you get out of that wet coat and
into a dry martini.

Robert Benchley in *The Major and the Minor*

— What would you like to have?
— Sex.

> Susan Anspach replies to George Segal in
> *Blume in Love*

☆

Oh, I don't know. I'm just a hack writer who drinks too much and falls in love with girls. You.

> Joseph Cotten in *The Third Man*

☆

I suppose you know you have a wonderful body. I'd like to do it in clay.

> Lola Allbright in *Champion*

☆

Come on darling. Why don't you kick off your spurs?

> Elizabeth Taylor to Rock Hudson in *Giant*

How can they give you a medal for a war
they don't even want you to fight?

Bruce Dern in *Coming Home*

☆

Mrs Robinson, you're trying to seduce me.
Aren't you?

Dustin Hoffman in *The Graduate*

☆

No matter what I ever do or say, Heathcliff,
this is me — now — standing on this hill
with you. This is me, forever.

Merle Oberon in *Wuthering Heights*

☆

He'll regret it to his dying day — if he ever
lives that long.

Victor McLaglen in *The Quiet Man*

— Jeez, you're old fashioned, aren't you?
— From the waist up.

> Charlotte Rampling being taken aback by Robert Mitchum in *Farewell My Lovely*

☆

My great-aunt Jennifer ate a whole box of candy every day of her life. She lived to be 102, and, when she had been dead for three days, she looked better than you do now.

> Monty Woolley in *The Man Who Came to Dinner*

☆

My religion? My dear, I'm a millionaire. That's my religion.

> Robert Morley in *Major Barbara*

☆

I like a man who can run faster than I can.

> Jane Russell to Marilyn Monroe in *Gentleman Prefer Blondes*

I'm a bagel on a plate of onion rolls.

> Barbara Streisand in *Funny Girl*

☆

I'm used to being top banana in the shock
department.

> Audrey Hepburn in *Breakfast at Tiffany's*

☆

I'm not the kind of man to take no answer
for an answer.

> Paul Ford in *The Teahouse of the August Moon*

☆

I wear the pants, and she beats me with the
belt.

> Edward G. Robinson in *All My Sons*

That was the most fun I've had without laughing.

Woody Allen awarding points to Diane Keaton
in *Annie Hall*

☆

Do you think (sex) will take the place of baseball?

Deborah Kerr in *An Affair to Remember*

☆

Don't you think it's better for a girl to be preoccupied with sex than occupied?

Maggie McNamara in *The Moon is Blue*

☆

They was giving *me* 10,000 watts a day, and, you know, I'm hot to that. The next woman takes me out is going to light up like a pinball machine and pay off in silver dollars.

Jack Nicholson in *One Flew Over the Cuckoo's Nest*

Heh, this may be the last chance I'll have to tell you to do anything, so I'm telling you: shut up.

Spencer Tracey in *Guess Who's Coming to Dinner*

☆

Shut up? You can't talk like that to me until after we're married.

Bob Hope in *Son of Paleface*

☆

Jenny's daughter is still going with that actor. An actor? Fashions in sin change. In my day, it was Englishmen.

Lucile Watson in *Watch on the Rhine*

☆

— I am troubled with insomnia.
— Well, I know a good cure for it.
— Yeah?
— Get plenty of sleep.

W.C.Fields humouring John Lipson in
Never Give a Sucker an Even Break

I love the smell of napalm in the morning ...
It smells like victory.

> Robert Duvall in *Apocalypse Now*

☆

If I smelled as bad as you, I wouldn't live
near people.

> Kim Darby in *True Grit*

☆

And I'll tell you another thing: frankly
you're beginning to smell — and, for a stud
in New York, that's a handicap.

> Dustin Hoffman to Jon Voight in
> *Midnight Cowboy*

☆

Well, if you look at it, it's a barn. If you
smell it, it's a stable.

> Groucho Marx in *Monkey Business*

Would you take your clammy hand off my chair? You have the touch of a love-starved cobra.

Monty Woolley in *The Man Who Came to Dinner*

☆

— He's not the man for you. I can see that, but I sorta like him. He's got a lot of charm.
— He comes by it naturally. His grandfather was a snake.

Rosalind Russell replying to Ralph Bellamy in
His Girl Friday

☆

You know the old story: when St Patrick drove the snakes out of Ireland, they swam to New York and joined the police force.

Frederic March in *The Iceman Cometh*

☆

A son is a poor substitute for a lover.

Anthony Perkins in *Psycho*

Oh Richard, it profits a man nothing to give his soul for the whole world — but for Wales?

Paul Schofield in *A Man For All Seasons*

☆

Did you ever hear a rhinoceros in labour?

Fred Astaire in *The Pleasure of his Company*

☆

Just listen to this stomach of mine. Way it sounds, you'd think I had a hyena inside me.

Humphrey Bogart in *African Queen*

☆

Look, it happens to everybody. I mean, I love your mother, but you know, sometimes you need a little stimulation, you know.

Richard Castellano in *Lovers and Other Strangers*

Let me tell you about making men strong: Einstein couldn't kick a football across this dance floor, but he changed the shape of the universe.

> Kirk Douglas in *A Letter to Three Wives*

☆

One more success like that, and I'll sell my body to a medical institute.

> Groucho Marx in *The Cocoanuts*

☆

Tell me, Mrs Wright, does your husband interfere with your marriage?

> Oscar Levant in *Humouresque*

☆

He *talked* like a Greek statue. I don't think he knew more than a dozen words — 'scotch and soda', and one or two more.

> Ingrid Bergman in *Indiscreet*

Only time a woman doesn't care to talk is when she's dead.

> William Demarest in
> *The Miracle of Morgan's Creek*

☆

With Nixon in the White House, good health seemed to be in bad taste.

> Jane Fonda in *California Suite*

☆

Hello. Is this someone with good news or money? No? Goodbye.

> Jason Robards in *A Thousand Clowns*

☆

There's nothing quite so mysterious and silent as a dark theatre. A night without a star.

> Grace Kelly in *The Country Girl*

We rob banks.

Warren Beatty in *Bonnie and Clyde*

☆

We have other prisoners, Captain: must I remind you that a chain is only as strong as its weakest link?

Richard Loo in *The Purple Heart*

☆

A man sentenced to life can always 'spare a few minutes'.

Humphrey Bogart in *We're No Angels*

☆

Here's to plain speaking and clear understanding.

Sydney Greenstreet in *The Maltese Falcon*

☆

Here's looking at you, kid.

Humphrey Bogart in *Casablanca*

Maybe we could do something else together,
Mrs Robinson, would you like to go to a
movie?

Dustin Hoffman in *The Graduate*

☆

Early to rise
And early to bed
Makes a man healthy
But socially dead

Alan Hale in *They Drive by Night*

☆

I feel as though somebody stepped on my
tongue with muddy feet.

W.C. Fields in *Never Give a Sucker an Even Break*

☆

I know you have a civil tongue in your head.
I sewed it there myself.

Whit Bissell in *I was a Teenage Frankenstein*

When I get in a tight spot, I shoot my way out of it. Why sure! Shoot first and argue afterwards. You know, this game ain't for guys that's soft.

> Edward G. Robinson in *Little Caesar*

☆

I'm not thin-skinned, Mr Shannon.

> Deborah Kerr in *The Night of Iguana*

☆

Adam Cook is my name. I'm a concert pianist. That's a pretentious way of saying I'm unemployed at the moment.

> Oscar Levant in *An American in Paris*

☆

That is a B, darling — the first letter of a seven letter word that means your late father.

> Rosalind Russell in *Auntie Mame*

— I always like redheads.
— You shouldn't. Red means stop.
— I'm colour-blind.

> George Raft in *They Drive by Night*

☆

A lot of women say no when they mean yes.

> Paul Newman in *The Long, Hot Summer*

☆

You know, it takes two to get one in trouble.

> Mae West in *She Done Him Wrong*

☆

Trouble with England, it's all pomp and no circumstance. You're very wise to get out of it, escape while you can.

> Humphrey Bogart *Beat the Devil*

Until you stirred him up, I had no trouble with God.

> William Powell in *Life with Father*

☆

The first thing to do is to make sure that he's dead. I don't trust him.

> Leo G. Carroll in *We're no Angels*

☆

I won't let myself fall in love with a man who won't trust me no matter what I might do.

> Marilyn Monroe in *Gentlemen Prefer Blondes*

☆

Sebastian said, 'Truth is the bottom of a bottomless well'.

> Katherine Hepburn in *Suddenly, Last Summer*

I was born ugly! Do you know how an ugly woman feels? Do you know what it is to be ugly all your life and to feel in here that you are beautiful?

> Katrina Paxinou in *For Whom the Bell Tolls*

☆

As many times as I'll be married, I'll never understand women.

> Tony Randall in *Pillow Talk*

☆

Now that was impertinent of him — to die with his rent unpaid.

> Basil Rathbone in *A Tale of Two Cities*

☆

Very stupid to kill the only servant in the house. Now we don't even know where to find the marmalade.

> Judith Anderson in *And Then There Were None*

He's the only man I know who can strut
sitting down.

Gene Kelly in *Inherit the Wind*

☆

The Korova milkbar sold milk — plus —
milk plus vellocet or synthemsc or drencrom
— which is what we are drinking. This
would sharpen you up and make you ready
for a bit of the old ultra-violence.

Malcolm McDowell in *A Clockwork Orange*

☆

I don't like violence, Tom. I'm a
businessman. Murder's a big expense.

Al Lettieri in *The Godfather*

☆

Mister, the stork that brought you must have
been a vulture.

Ann Sheridan in *Torrid Zone*

Well, I suppose we'll have to feed the duchess. Even vultures have to eat.

Shirley MacLaine in *The Children's Hour*

☆

She came at me in sections. More curves than the scenic railway.

Fred Astaire in *The Band Wagon*

☆

No mob ever wants justice. They want vengeance.

Peter Ustinov in *Quo Vadis*

☆

Look at that! Look how she moves! That's just like jello on springs. She's got some sort of built-in motor or something, huh? I tell you it's a whole different sex.

Jack Lemmon on Marilyn Monroe in
Some Like It Hot

I want you to be a merry widower.

Ali McGraw in *Love Story*

☆

Cry? I never knew a woman that size had
that much water in her.

Tony Randall in *Pillow Talk*

☆

That's it, baby! When you got it, flaunt it!
Flaunt it!

Zero Mostel in *The Producers*

☆

Rick, you should have shot that fella a long
time ago. Now, he's too rich to kill.

Chill Wills in *Giant*

☆

Are you mountainously rich?

Vanessa Redgrave in *Isadora*

With all the unrest in the world, I don't
think anybody should have a yacht that
sleeps more than twelve.

> Tony Curtis in *Some Like It Hot*

☆

Why don't you bore a hole in yourself and
let the sap run out.

> Groucho Marx in *Horse Feathers*

☆

— Why is it that women always think they
understand men better than men do?
— Maybe because they live with them.

> William Holden and Grace Kelly in
> *The Country Girl*

☆

Why is it that a woman always thinks that
the most savage thing she can say to a man is
to impugn his cockmanship.

> William Holden in *Network*

Why anyone would want to live anywhere but Hong Kong I can't understand. Where else in the world could you get ten servants for the price of one.

Isobel Elsom in *Love is a Many-Splendored Thing*

☆

The Reverend Mother always says when the Lord closes a door somewhere, he opens a window.

Julie Andrews in *The Sound of Music*

☆

That's what I always say. Love flies out the door when money comes inuendo.

Groucho Marx in *Monkey Business*

☆

It is widely held that too much wine will check a man's desire. Indeed, it will — in a dull man.

Michael MacLiammoir in *Tom Jones*

She insisted upon diving into the pool. And, when she hit the water, the wine hit her.

Frank Sinatra in *High Society*

☆

They all start out as Juliets and end up as Lady Macbeths.

William Holden in *The Country Girl*

☆

Six wives — and the best of them was the worst.

Charles Laughton in
The Private Life of Henry VIII

☆

I've had five wives already. One more or less makes no difference to me.

Charlie Chaplin in *Limelight*

Buried three of 'em. Good women, bad
diets.

Arthur Hunnicutt in Harry and Tonto

☆

'She's got the three things that really matter
in a wife', everyone said, 'breeding, brains
and beauty.' And I believed them
completely. But I never had a moment's
happiness with her. She was incapable of
love, or kindness, or decency.

Laurence Olivier in Rebecca

☆

Women make the best psychoanalysts till
they fall in love. After that, they make the
best patients.

Michael Chekhov in Spellbound

☆

I don't use a pen. I write with a goose quill
dipped in venom.

Clifton Wess in Laura

When women go wrong, men go right after them.

> Mae West in *She Done Him Wrong*

☆

We older men supply the champagne —
but, when youth sings, the old fool stays
home and pays the piper.

> Lionel Barrymore in *Mata Hari*

☆

Fred Astaire
After his screen test the verdict was:
'Can't act. Slightly bald. Can dance a little.'

☆

Lauren Bacall
At Humphrey Bogart's funeral, she placed a
small gold whistle in the urn with his ashes.
It was inscribed 'If you want anything, just
whistle' which were the lines she spoke to
him in their first film together *To Have and
Have Not*.

Tallulah Bankhead
At the opening night party for *The Little Foxes* in which she starred, Dashiel Hammet commented on Bankhead's addiction to cocaine: 'You don't know what you're talking about. I tell you cocaine isn't habit forming and I know because I've been taking it for years!'

☆

Robert Benchley (1889-1945)
On visiting Venice for the first time, he sent the following telegram to Harold Ross, editor of The New Yorker:
'Streets full of water. Please advise.'

☆

At a Hollywood party guests had to write their own epitaphs. A notorious actress who'd had several marriages and affairs appeared stumped. Benchley wrote: 'At last she sleeps alone.'

Sir Noel Coward
At a second night of a play centred on a
fourteen-year-old prodigy, he remarked:
'Two things should have been cut. The
second act and that youngster's throat.'

☆

Zsa Zsa Gabor
'I'm breaking my engagement to a very
wealthy man who has already given me a
sable coat, diamonds, a store and a Rolls
Royce. What should I do?'
'Give back the store,' advised Zsa Zsa.

☆

Sam Goldwyn
'I am willing to admit that I may not always
be right, but I am never wrong.'

☆

There was a fuss with another studio chief
over an actor. Arbitration was suggested to
resolve the dispute. Goldwyn agreed
reluctantly: 'Okay, as long as it's understood
that I get him.'

'I'll give you a definite maybe.'

☆

David Selznick was alarmed by a midnight call from Sam Goldwyn: 'David you and I are in terrible trouble.'

Selznick pondered but couldn't think why and so asked Goldwyn — 'You've got Gable, and I want him' replied Goldwyn.

☆

Sir Alfred Hitchcock
The customs officer at a French airport looked suspiciously at Hitchcock's passport in which his occupation was listed simply as a Producer: 'What do you produce?' he asked.

'Gooseflesh' came Hitchcock's reply.

☆

Judy Holliday
The actress found herself being chased around the room by a lecherous studio hand. To satisfy him, she put her hand inside her dress and pulled out her falsies: 'Here, I think this is what you want.'

Bob Hope

'The hotel room where I'm staying is so small that the rats are round shouldered.'

There then followed a complaint from the proprietor, after which and, to avoid damages, he responded, 'I'm sorry I said that the rats in that hotel were round-shouldered. They're not.'

☆

Wilfred Hyde-White

A horse-lover, he was to be found in the bankruptcy court, explaining his predicament, the official receiver was none too pleased with his efforts: 'Mr Hyde-White, if you cannot tell us how you spent such a large sum in so short a time, perhaps you could tell us who will win the Gold Cup at Ascot this afternoon ...?'

'Of course, dear fellow' (naming the eventual winner) 'but, only have a small bet, we don't want to have to change places do we?'

Chico Marx

Marx's wife had caught him kissing a chorus girl. During the ensuing row, Chico declared 'I wasn't kissing her. I was whispering in her mouth.'

☆

A new neighbour, failing to recognize Chico, asked him what he did for a living: 'I'm a smuggler. Nothing big, just Mexicans.'

☆

Groucho Marx

Groucho was gardening in tattered clothes. A wealthy matron in a Cadillac spotted him and pondered wondering if he could possibly work for her: 'Gardener, how much does the lady of the house pay you?'

'Oh, I don't get paid in dollars. The lady of the house lets me sleep with her.'

A drunk accosted Groucho, slapped him on the back and said — 'You old son-of-a-gun, you probably don't remember me.'

Marx looked at him: 'I never forget a face, but in your case I'll be glad to make an exception.'

☆

Groucho disliked producer Harry Cohn who worked for Columbia Pictures. With Chico, he viewed Cohn's latest film. When the words 'Columbia Pictures presents' came up on the screen, Groucho turned to Chico and said: 'Drags, doesn't it.'

☆

Victor Mature
Mature applied for membership to the Los Angeles Country Club only to be told 'We don't accept actors'.

'I'm no actor' Mature replied 'and I've sixty-four pictures to prove it.'

Louis B. Mayer
Mayer's funeral was attended by huge crowds but not necessarily because of his popularity. As his one-time partner, Sam Goldwyn, put it: 'The reason so many showed up was because they wanted to make sure he was dead.'

☆

Dorothy Parker
Harold Ross, editor of The New Yorker, began pressing Dorothy for her copy even though she'd been on her honeymoon. Typically she replied: 'Too fucking busy, and vice versa.'

☆

Dorothy was told that a certain London actress had broken a leg: 'How terrible, she must have done it sliding down a barrister.'

☆

Writing a note on a Yale prom full of local beauties; she wrote: 'If all those sweet young things were laid end to end, I wouldn't be at all surprised.'

David O. Selznick
There are only two classes — first class and
no class.

☆

Spencer Tracey
When asked what he looked for in a script,
he replied: 'Days off'.

☆

Eli Wallach
At the opening on Broadway of *Luv*,
Wallach gazed at the queue at the box office:
'There's something about a crowd that
brings a lump to my wallet.'

☆

Jack Warner
Field Marshall Montgomery visited
Hollywood and Sam Goldwyn gave a party
for him. Welcoming him, he opened with:
'It gives me great pleasure to welcome a very
distinguished soldier. Ladies and
gentlemen, I propose a vote to Marshall
Field Montgomery.'

Jack Warner responded quickly with the
retort: 'You mean Montgomery Ward.'

Warner usually took a nap in the afternoon and he was not to be disturbed. Bette Davis burst into the office while Warner was asleep and began ranting about a script that clearly upset her.

Without opening his eyes, Warner reached for the phone and called his secretary: 'Come in and wake me up, I'm having a nightmare.'

☆

Billy Wilder
Assigned to Berlin at the end of the Second World War to help re-establish the German industry, Wilder authorized the resumption of the Oberammergau Passion Play. He was faced with a sensitive problem, would he let a supporter of the Nazi's play Christ.

'Certainly', Wilder responded, 'if you've real nails.'

☆

Wilder was asked which was his own favourite film. '*Some Like it Hot*' came the retort. The journalist wondered why he hadn't chosen one of his classics like *Sunset Boulevard* or *Witness for the Prosecution*.

'They are nice little pictures, but in those days, I wasn't getting a percentage of the gross.'

☆

Michael Wilding
He was asked if actors had any features that set them apart from other human beings.
'You can pick out actors by the glazed look that comes into their eyes when the conversation wanders away from themselves.'

☆

Kiss me, my fool.

Theda Bara in *A Fool There Was*

☆

Harness my zebras.

Jacqueline Wogan in *King of Kings*

You ain't heard nothin' yet.

> Al Jolson in *The Jazz Singer*

☆

Elementary, my dear Watson.

> Clive Brook as Sherlock Holmes in
> *The Return of Sherlock Holmes*

☆

You dirty, double-crossing rat.

> James Cagney in *Blonde Crazy*

☆

I am walking alone because I want to be alone.

> Greta Garbo in *The Single Standard*

☆

Here's another fine mess you've gotten me into.

> Oliver Hardy to Stan Laurel

The things I've done for England.

Charles Laughton in
The Private Life of Henry VIII

☆

We have ways of making men talk.

Douglas Douglas in *The Lives of a Bengal Lancer*

☆

We have ways and means of making you
talk.

Nazi to Anna Neagle in *Odette*

☆

Play it again, Sam.

Credited to Humphrey Bogart in *Casablanca* but
in fact the lines go:—

Ilsa: Play it once, Sam, for old time's sake.
Sam: Ah don't know what you mean, Miss
Ilsa.
Ilsa: Play it, Sam. Play 'As Time Goes By'.

Play it again, Sam.

Woody Allen's film, 1972.

☆

Here's looking at you kid.

Humphrey Bogart in *Casablanca*

☆

A man's gotta do, what a man's gotta do.

Credited to Alan Ladd in *Shane* but he actually said:

A man has to be what he is Joey.

☆

That's the way, the cookie crumbles.

Credited to Jack Lemmon in *The Apartment* except his riposte was:

Yeah, well, that's the way it crumbles, cookie-wise.

It's all part of life's rich pageant.

> Peter Sellers in *A Shot in the Dark*

☆

I'm going to make him an offer he can't refuse.

> Marlon Brando in *The Godfather*

☆

Come with me to the Casbah.

> Credited, but not said, by Charles Boyer in
> *Algiers*

☆

In Italy, for thirty years under the Borgias, they had warfare, terror, murder and bloodshed, but they produced Michelangelo, Leonardo de Vinci and the Renaissance. In Switzerland, they had brotherly love; they have five hundred years of democracy and peace — and what did that produce? The cuckoo clock.

> Orson Welles in *The Third Man*

Tara! Home! I'll go home, and I'll think of some way to get him back. After all, tomorrow is another day.

Vivien Leigh in *Gone With The Wind*

☆

So I want you to get up now. I want all of you to get up out of your chairs. I want you to get up right now and go to the window, open it and stick your head out and yell, I'm as mad as hell, and I'm not going to take this anymore.

Peter Finch in *Network*

☆

Because it seemed like a good idea at the time.

Richard Barthelmess in *The Last Flight*

☆

Would you be shocked if I put on something more comfortable?

Jean Harlow in *Hell's Angels*

Not only is there no God, but try getting a plumber on weekends.

Woody Allen in *Getting Even*

☆

Hindsight is always 20:20

Billy Wilder

☆

I believe in sex and death — two experiences that come once in a lifetime.

Woody Allen in *Sleeper*

☆

With Her Majesty, life is one eternal glass of milk.

Martita Hunt in *Anastasia*

☆

Oh, I'm eternally right. But what good does it do me?

Leslie Howard in *The Petrified Forest*

A life that is planned is a closed life ... It can be endured, perhaps. It cannot be liked.

Robert Donat in *The Inn of the Sixth Happiness*

☆

If your head says one thing and your whole life says another, your head always loses.

Humphrey Bogart in *Key Largo*

☆

Give a man a free hand and he'll run it all over you.

Mae West

☆

Basically my wife was immature. I'd be at home in the bath and she'd come in and sink my boats.

Woody Allen

A relationship I think is like a shark. You know it has to constantly move forward or it dies.

Woody Allen in *Annie Hall*

☆

Husbands are like fires — they go out when unattended.

Zsa Zsa Gabor

☆

It's an extra dividend when you like the girl you're in love with.

Clark Gable

☆

Love conquers all things except poverty and toothache.

Mae West

Success is a public affair. Failure is a private funeral.

Rosalind Russell

☆

I'm going under. I'm being sunk by a society that demands success when all I can offer is failure.

Zero Mostel in *The Producers*

☆

I coulda had class! I coulda been a contender! I coulda been somebody! Instead of a bum which is what I am!

Marlon Brando in *On The Waterfront*

☆

Fifty — the old age of youth and the youth of old age.

William Powell in *Mr Peabody and The Mermaid*

Failure is a highly contagious disease.

Paul Newman in *Sweet Bird of Youth*

☆

It's sad to grow old, but nice to ripen.

Brigitte Bardot in *Nova*

☆

God is a living doll.

Jane Russell in *Esquire*

☆

There is nothing more old-fashioned than being-up-to-date.

Noel Coward in *The Observer*

☆

Life is a concentration camp. You're stuck here and there's no way out and you can only rage impotently against your persecutors.

Woody Allen in *Esquire*

It's not that I'm afraid to die. I just don't want to be there when it happens.

Woody Allen in *Newsweek*

☆

She tells enough white lies to ice a cake.

Dorothy Parker

☆

She runs the gamut of emotions from A to B.

Dorothy Parker on Katherine Hepburn

☆

Dorothy Parker hearing that Clare Boothe Luce was frequently kind to her inferiors: And where does she find them?

☆

An angel, with spurs.

Joe Pasternak on Judy Garland

A vacuum with nipples.

Otto Preminger on Marilyn Monroe

☆

Most of the time he sounds like he has a
mouth full of wet toilet paper.

Rex Reed on Marlon Brando

☆

Anyone who goes to a psychiatrist should
have his head examined.

Sam Goldwyn

☆

The film is a machine for seeing more than
meets the eye.

Iris Barry

☆

Cinema is death in action.

Jean Cocteau

Let's have some new cliches.

Sam Goldwyn

☆

From a polite conference comes a polite
movie.

Sam Goldwyn

☆

What we want is a story that starts with an
earthquake and works its way up to a
climax.

Sam Goldwyn

☆

I can answer you in two words — Im
Possible.

Sam Goldwyn

☆

Drama is life with the dull bits cut out.

Alfred Hitchcock

American motion pictures are written by the half-educated for the half-witted.

St. John Irvine

☆

A film is never really good unless the camera is an eye in the head of a poet.

Orson Welles

☆

A movie studio is the best toy a boy ever had.

Orson Welles

☆

A movie without sex would be like a candy bay without nuts.

Earl Wilson

An actor's a guy who if you ain't talkin'
about him, ain't listening.

Marlon Brando

☆

Actors are crap.

John Ford

☆

The best screen actor is that man who can
do nothing extremely well.

Alfred Hitchcock

☆

Acting is just one big bag of tricks.

Laurence Olivier

☆

The art of acting consists in keeping people
from coughing.

Ralph Richardson

A critic is a bundle of biases held loosely together by a sense of taste.

Whitney Balliett

☆

A good review from the critics is just another stay of execution.

Dustin Hoffman.

☆

A critic is a legless man who teaches running.

Channing Pollock

☆

A critic is a man who knows the way but can't drive a car.

Kenneth Tynan

I believe in censorship. After all, I made a fortune out of it.

Mae West

☆

There goes the good time that was had by all.

Bette Davis

☆

I have a perfect cure for a sore throat — cut it.

Alfred Hitchcock

☆

Bisexuality immediately doubles your chances of a date on Saturday night.

Woody Allen, *New York Herald Tribune*

Love is the answer, but while you are waiting for the answer, sex raises some pretty good questions.

Woody Allen, *New York Herald Tribune*

☆

It's the good girls who keep the diaries; the bad girls never have the time.

Tallulah Bankhead

☆

Anyone who says he can see through women is missing a lot.

Groucho Marx

☆

Whoever named it necking was a poor judge of anatomy.

Groucho Marx

The first girl you go to bed with is *always* pretty.

> Walter Matthau

☆

Sex is an emotion in motion.

> Mae West

☆

I'm a late bloomer. My mind and my experience have caught up to my body.

> Raquel Welch

☆

The trouble with the world is that everybody in it, is three drinks behind.

> Humphrey Bogart

☆

You're not drunk if you can lie on the floor without holding on.

> Dean Martin

I was T.T. until prohibition.

Groucho Marx

☆

The only reason that cocaine is such a rage today is that people are too dumb and lazy to get themselves together to roll a joint.

Jack Nicholson

☆

Bad taste is simply saying the truth before it should be said.

Mel Brooks

☆

Style is self-plagiarism.

Alfred Hitchcock

☆

I always was an independent, even when I had partners.

Sam Goldwyn

I can't play a loser — I don't look like one.

Rock Hudson

☆

There used to be a me, but I had it surgically removed.

Peter Sellers

☆

I used to be snow white ... but I drifted.

Mae West

☆

A verbal contract isn't worth the paper it's written on.

Sam Goldwyn

☆

Anyone who lives within his means suffers from a lack of imagination.

Lionel Stander

There's a broad with her future behind her.

Constance Bennett on Marilyn Monroe

☆

Chaplin is no businessman — all he knows
is that he can't take anything less.

Sam Goldwyn on Charlie Chaplin

☆

I'm the truck driver, he's the aristocrat.

Gene Kelly on Fred Astaire

☆

A deer in the body of a woman, living
resentfully in the Hollywood zoo.

Clare Booth Luce on Greta Garbo

☆

Wayne has an endless face and he can go on
forever.

Louis B. Meyer on John Wayne

In America sex is an obsession, in other parts of the world it is fact.

Marlene Dietrich

☆

Hollywood money isn't money. It's congealed snow.

Dorothy Parker

☆

The only 'ism' Hollywood believes in is plagiarism.

Dorothy Parker

☆

Hollywood's all right, it's the pictures that are bad.

Orson Welles

Hollywood is an extraordinary kind of temporary place.

John Schlesinger

☆

This makes me so sore it gets my dandruff up.

Sam Goldwyn

☆

If only God would give me some clear sign! Like making a large deposit in my name at a Swiss bank.

Woody Allen

☆

A woman drove me to drink and I never even had the courtesy to thank her.

W. C. Fields

What contemptible scoundrel stole the cork
from my lunch?

W. C. Fields

☆

If at first you don't succeed, try, try, again.
Then quit. There's no use being a dam fool
about it.

W. C. Fields

☆

He's the kind of man who picks his friends
— to pieces.

Mae West

☆

When choosing between two evils, I always
like to try the one I've never tried before.

Mae West

I never hated a man enough to give him his diamonds back.

Zsa Zsa Gabor

☆

There's one way to find out if a man is honest — ask him. If he says 'Yes', you know he is a crook.

Groucho Marx

☆

I do not believe in an after life, although I am bringing a change of underwear.

Woody Allen

☆

I don't want to achieve immortality through my work, I want to achieve it through not dying.

Woody Allen

It ain't no sin if you crack a few laws now and then, just so long as you don't break any.

Mae West

☆

I never loved another person the way I loved myself

Mae West

☆

Marriage is a great institution, but I'm not ready for an institution, yet.

Mae West

☆

Military intelligence is a contradiction in terms.

Groucho Marx

Military justice is to justice what military music is to music.

Groucho Marx

☆

I am free of all prejudices. I hate everyone equally.

W. C. Fields

☆

Most of the time I don't have much fun. The rest of the time I don't have any fun at all.

Woody Allen

☆

You can include me out.

Sam Goldwyn

☆

One more drink and I'd be under the host.

Dorothy Parker

— When I was at the age of fourteen I had seven men under me.
— Were you working in a cemetery?

Groucho Marx to a businessman

☆

Gluttony is not a secret vice.

Orson Welles

☆

Education bewildered me with knowledge and facts in which I was only mildly interested.

Charlie Chaplin

☆

I had to marry a virgin — I hate criticism.

Klaus Maria Brandau in *Out of Africa*

☆

A man in the house is worth two in the street.

Mae West

Women are as old as they feel — and men are old when they lose their feelings.

Mae West

☆

If you want to see a comic strip, you should see me in a shower.

Groucho Marx to a cartoonist

☆

I met my wife on a ferry boat, and when we landed she gave me the ship.

Groucho Marx to a marriage broker

☆

I *thought* you looked down in the mouth.

Groucho Marx to a dentist

☆

— When a boy kisses a girl and she says 'Stop', usually she means, 'Stop it. I love it'. And it was sort of like that.
— You mean when a girl says 'Stop' she

really means 'Don't stop'? Boy, the nights I've wasted. I was always so gullible.

Groucho Marx to an amorous admirer

☆

— My brother and I own a business called Up and Atom.
— Well, what is it? A breakfast cereal with fallout?

Groucho Marx to a businessman

☆

— What does a girl think when she meets a handsome boy?
— Oh, I imagine she thinks about the same thing boys do.
— You mean girls too wonder if they'll be drafted?

Groucho Marx to Coco

FILMS AND SCREENWRITERS

An Affair To Remember Screenplay by Delmer
Daves and Leo McCarey; based on an
original story by Mildred Cram and Leo
McCarey.

The African Queen Screenplay by James Agee
and John Huston; based on the novel by
C.S. Forester.

Algiers Screenplay by John Howard Lawson
and James M. Cain; based on *Pepe le Moko*,
a novel by Detective Ashelbe.

All About Eve Screenplay by Joseph L.
Mankiewicz based on "The Wisdom of
Eve," a radio play and short story by Mary
Orr.

All My Sons Screenplay by Chester Erskine;
based on the play by Arthur Miller.

All Quiet on the Western Front Screenplay by
Dell Andrews, Maxwell Anderson, and
George Abbott; based on the novel by
Erich Maria Remarque.

All the King's Men Screenplay by Robert
Rossen; based on the novel by Robert
Penn Warren.

An American in Paris Original Screenplay by
Alan Jay Lerner.

Anastasia Screenplay by Arthur Laurents;
based on the play by Marcelle Maurette
and Broadway adaptation by Guy Bolton.

And Then There Were None Screenplay by
Dudley Nichols; based on *Ten Little
Indians*, a play and novel by Agatha
Christie.

Animal Crackers Screenplay by Morrie
Ryskind; based on the musical play by
George S. Kaufman and Morrie Ryskind.

Annie Hall Original Screenplay by Woody
Allen and Marshall Brickman.

The Apartment Original Screenplay by Billy
Wilder and I.A.L. Diamond.

Apocalypse Now Screenplay by John Milius and
Francis Ford Coppola.

Arsenic and Old Lace Screenplay by Julius J.
Epstein and Philip G. Epstein; based on
the play by Joseph Kesselring.

Auntie Mame Screenplay by Betty Comden and
Adolph Green; based on the play by

Jerome Lawrence and Robert E. Lee and novel by Patrick Dennis.

The Bachelor and the Bobby-Soxer Original Screenplay by Sidney Sheldon.

The Bachelor Party Screenplay by Paddy Chayefsky.

The Bad and the Beautiful Screenplay by Charles Schnee; based on two short stories by George Bradshaw.

The Band Wagon Original Screenplay by Betty Comden and Adolph Green.

Barefoot in the Park Screenplay by Neil Simon; based on his play.

Beat the Devil Screenplay by John Huston and Truman Capote; based on the novel by James Helvick.

The Big Carnival, a.k.a. *Ace in the Hole* Original Screenplay by Billy Wilder, Lesser Samuels, and Walter Newman.

The Big Sleep Screenplay by William Faulkner, Leigh Brackett, and Jules Furthman; based on the novel by Raymond Chandler.

Blume in Love Original Screenplay by Paul Mazursky.

Bonnie and Clyde Original Screenplay by David Newman and Robert Benton.

Breakfast at Tiffany's Screenplay by George Axelrod; based on the novella by Truman Capote.

The Bridge on the River Kwai Screenplay by Pierre Boulle; based on his novel, *The Bridge Over the River Kwai*.

The Caine Mutiny Screenplay by Stanley Roberts; additional dialogue by Michael Blankfort; based on the novel by Herman Wouk.

California Suite Screenplay by Neil Simon; based on his play.

Casablanca Screenplay by Julius J. Epstein, Philip G. Epstein and Howard Koch; based on *Everybody Comes to Rick's*, a play by Murray Burnett and Joan Alison.

The Cat and the Canary Screenplay by Walter De Leon and Lynn Starling; based on the play by John Willard.

Cat on a Hot Tin Roof Screenplay by Richard

Brooks and James Poe; based on the play by Tennessee Williams.

Catch-22 Screenplay by Buck Henry; based on the novel by Joseph Heller.

The Chalk Garden Screenplay by John Michael Hayes; based on the play by Enid Bagnold.

Champion Screenplay by Carl Foreman; based on the short story by Ring Lardner.

The Children's Hour Screenplay by John Michael Hayes; adaptation by Lillian Hellman; based on her play.

Citizen Kane Original Screenplay by Herman J. Mankiewicz and Orson Welles.

Claudine Original Screenplay by Tina Pine and Lester Pine.

A Clockwork Orange Screenplay by Stanley Kubrick; based on the novel by Anthony Burgess.

The Cocoanuts Screenplay by Morrie Ryskind; based on the musical play by George S. Kaufman and Morrie Ryskind.

Coming Home Screenplay by Waldo Salt and

Robert C. Jones; based on a story by Nancy Dowd.

The Country Girl Screenplay by George Seaton; based on the play by Clifford Odets.

The Dark at the Top of the Stairs Screenplay by Irving Ravetch and Harriet Frank Jr.; based on the play by William Inge.

Darling Original Screenplay by Frederic Raphael.

A Day at the Races Screenplay by Robert Pirosh, George Seaton, and George Oppenheimer; based on a story by Robert Pirosh and George Seaton.

Desk Set Screenplay by Phoebe Ephron and Henry Ephron; based on *The Desk Set*, a play by William Marchant.

Detective Story Screenplay by Philip Yordan and Robert Wyler; based on the play by Sidney Kingsley.

Dracula Screenplay by Garrett Fort; based on the play by Hamilton Deane and John L. Balderston and novel by Bram Stoker.

Dragon Seed Screenplay by Marguerite Roberts

and Jane Murfin; based on the novel by
Pearl S. Buck.

Duck Soup Screenplay by Bert Kalmar and
Harry Ruby; additional dialogue by
Arthur Sheekman and Nat Perrin.

East of Eden Screenplay by Paul Osborn; based
on the novel by John Steinbeck.

The Electric Horseman Screenplay by Robert
Garland; based on a screen story by Paul
Gaer and Robert Garland and story by
Shelly Burton.

Farewell, My Lovely Screenplay by David Zelag
Goodman; based on the novel by
Raymond Chandler.

Female on the Beach Screenplay by Robert Hill
and Richard Alan Simmons; based on *The
Besieged Heart*, a play by Robert Hill.

For Whom the Bell Tolls Screenplay by Dudley
Nichols; based on the novel by Ernest
Hemingway.

42nd Street Screenplay by Rian James and
James Seymour; based on the novel by
Bradford Ropes.

From Here to Eternity Screenplay by Daniel

Taradash; based on the novel by James
Jones.

Funny Girl Screenplay by Isobel Lennart;
based on her musical play.

Gentlemen Prefer Blondes Screenplay by Charles
Lederer; based on the musical play by
Joseph Fields and Anita Loos and novel by
Anita Loos.

The Ghost Breakers Screenplay by Walter De
Leon; based on "The Ghost Breaker", a
play by Paul Dickey and Charles W.
Goddard.

Gigi Screenplay by Alan Jay Lerner; based on
the novel by Colette.

Go West, Young Man Screenplay by Mae West;
based on *Personal Appearance*, a play by
Lawrence Riley.

The Go-Between Screenplay by Harold Pinter;
based on the novel by L. P. Hartley.

The Godfather Screenplay by Mario Puzo and
Francis Ford Coppola; based on the novel
by Mario Puzo.

Going My Way Screenplay by Frank Butler and

Frank Cavett; based on an original story by Leo McCarey.

Gone With The Wind Screenplay by Sidney Howard; based on the novel by Margaret Mitchell.

The Graduate Screenplay by Calder Willingham and Buck Henry; based on the novel by Charles Webb.

Grand Hotel Screenplay by William A. Drake; based on the play and novel by Vicki Baum.

The Grasshopper Screenplay by Jerry Belson and Garry Marshall; based on *The Passing of Evil*, a novel by Mark McShane.

The Green Berets Screenplay by James Lee Barrett; based on the novel by Robin Moore.

Guess Who's Coming To Dinner Original Screenplay by William Rose.

Hail The Conquering Hero Original Screenplay by Preston Sturges.

Harper Screenplay by William Goldman; based on the novel by J. Ross Macdonald.

Harry and Tonto Original Screenplay by Paul Mazursky and Josh Greenfeld.

The Hasty Heart Screenplay by Ranald MacDougall; based on the play by John Patrick.

The Heat's On Original Screenplay by Fitzroy Davis, George S. George, and Fred Schiller.

Hell's Angels Screenplay by Joseph Moncure March.

High Society Screenplay by John Patrick; based on *The Philadelphia Story*, a screenplay by Donald Ogden Stewart and play by Philip Barry.

His Girl Friday Screenplay by Charles Lederer; based on *The Front Page*, a play by Ben Hecht and Charles MacArthur.

Hondo Screenplay by James Edward Grant; based on "The Gift of Cochise", a short story by Louis L'Amour.

Horse Feathers Screenplay by Bert Kalmar, Harry Ruby, S.J. Perelman, and Will B. Johnstone.

How Green Was My Valley Screenplay by Philip

Dunne; based on the novel by Richard
Llewellyn.

Humoresque Screenplay by Clifford Odets and
Zachary Gold; based on a short story by
Fannie Hurst.

I Was a Teenage Frankenstein Original
Screenplay by Kenneth Langtry.

I'll Never Forget Whatshisname Screenplay by
Peter Draper.

I'm No Angel Screenplay and dialogue by Mae
West; story suggestions by Lowell
Brentano; continuity by Harlan
Thompson.

The Iceman Cometh Screenplay based on the
play by Eugene O'Neill.

Indiscreet Screenplay by Norman Krasna;
based on his play, *Kind Sir*.

Inherit the Wind Screenplay by Nathan E.
Douglas and Harold Jacob Smith; based
on the play by Jerome Lawrence and
Robert E. Lee.

The Inn of the Sixth Happiness Screenplay by
Isobel Lennart; based on *The Small
Woman*, a book by Alan Burgess.

Isadora Screenplay by Melvyn Bragg and Clive Exton; additional dialogue by Margaret Drabble; adaptation by Melvyn Bragg; based on the books, *My Life* by Isadora Duncan and *Isadora Duncan, an Intimate Portrait* by Sewell Stokes.

It Happened One Night Screenplay by Robert Riskin; based on "Night Bus", a short story by Samuel Hopkins Adams.

Joe Original Screenplay by Norman Wexler.

June Bride Screenplay by Ranald MacDougall; based on *Feature for June*, a play by Eileen Tighe and Graeme Lorimer.

Key Largo Screenplay by Richard Brooks and John Huston; based on the play by Maxwell Anderson.

King Kong Screenplay by James Creelman and Ruth Rose; based on an original story by Merian C. Cooper and Edgar Wallace.

King of Kings Screenplay by Philip Yordan.

Kings Row Screenplay by Casey Robinson; based on the novel by Henry Bellamann.

Klondike Annie Screenplay and dialogue by

Mae West; additional material suggested by Frank Mitchell.

The Late George Apley Screenplay by Philip Dunne; based on the play by John P. Marquand and George S. Kaufman and novel by John P. Marquand.

Laura Screenplay by Jay Dratler, Samuel Hoffenstein, and Betty Reinhardt; based on the novel by Vera Caspary.

Lawrence of Arabia Screenplay by Robert Bolt; based on *The Seven Pillars of Wisdom*, the autobiography of T.E. Lawrence.

A Letter to Three Wives Screenplay by Joseph L. Mankiewicz; adaptation by Vera Caspary; based on "One of Our Hearts", a short story by John Klempner.

Life With Father Screenplay by Donald Ogden Stewart; based on the play by Howard Lindsay and Russel Crouse and stories by Clarence Day Jr.

Limelight Original Screenplay by Charles Chaplin.

Little Caesar Screenplay by Francis Edwards Faragoh; based on the novel by W.R. Burnett.

The Lives of a Bengal Lancer Screenplay by
Waldemar Young, Achmed Abdullah,
John F. Balderston, Grover Jones and
William Slavens Monutt.

The Long, Hot Summer Screenplay by Irving
Ravetch and Harriet Frank Jr.; based on
The Hamlet, a novel by William Faulkner,
and "Barn Burning" and "The Spotted
Horses", two short stories by William
Faulkner.

Love Is a Many-Splendored Thing Screenplay by
John Patrick; based on *A Many-Splendored
Thing*, a novel by Han Suyin.

Love Story Original Screenplay by Erich Segal.

Lovers and Other Strangers Screenplay by Renee
Taylor, Joseph Bologna, and David Z.
Goodman; based on the play by Renee
Taylor and Joseph Bologna.

The Major and the Minor Screenplay by Charles
Brackett and Billy Wilder; based on *Connie
Goes Home*, a play by Edward Childs
Carpenter, and "Sunny Goes Home", a
short story by Fannie Kilbourne.

Major Barbara Screenplay by George Bernard
Shaw; based on his play.

Make Way for Tomorrow Screenplay by Vina
Delmar; based on the play by Helen Leary
and Nolan Leary and *The Years Are So
Long*, a novel by Josephine Lawrence.

The Maltese Falcon Screenplay by John
Huston; based on the novel by Dashiell
Hammett.

Mame Screenplay by Paul Zindel; based on the
musical play by Jerome Lawrence, Robert
E. Lee, and Jerry Herman and *Auntie
Mame*, a play by Jerome Lawrence and
Robert E. Lee, and novel by Patrick
Dennis.

A Man for All Seasons Screenplay by Robert
Bolt; based on his play.

The Man Who Came to Dinner Screenplay by
Julius J. Epstein and Philip G. Epstein;
based on the play by George S. Kaufman
and Moss Hart.

Mary, Mary Screenplay by Richard L. Breen;
based on the play by Jean Kerr.

Mata Hari Original Screenplay by Benjamin
Glazer and Leo Birinski; dialogue by
Doris Anderson and Gilbert Emery.

Midnight Cowboy Screenplay by Waldo Salt;

based on the novel by James Leo Herlihy.

The Miracle of Morgan's Creek Original
Screenplay by Preston Sturges.

Mr. Peabody and the Mermaid Screenplay by
Nunnally Johnson; based on *Peabody's
Mermaid*, a novel by Guy Jones and
Constance Jones.

Monkey Business Screenplay by S.J. Perelman
and Will B. Johnstone.

The Moon Is Blue Screenplay by F. Hugh
Herbert; based on his play.

Moulin Rouge Screenplay by Anthony Veiller
and John Huston; based on the novel by
Pierre La Mure.

Murder, My Sweet Screenplay by John Paxton;
based on *Farewell, My Lovely*, a novel by
Raymond Chandler.

My Darling Clementine Screenplay by Samuel
G. Engel and Winston Miller; based on a
story by Sam Hellman and *Wyatt Earp,
Frontier Marshal*, a book by Stuart N. Lake.

My Favorite Wife Screenplay by Bella Spewack
and Samuel Spewack; based on a story by

Bella Spewack, Samuel Spewack, and Leo McCarey.

My Reputation Screenplay by Catherine Turney; based on *Instruct My Sorrows*, a novel by Clare Jaynes.

Network Original Screenplay by Paddy Chayefsky.

Never Give a Sucker an Even Break Screenplay by John T. Neville and Prescott Chaplin; based on an original story by Otis Criblecoblis, a.k.a. W.C. Fields.

Night After Night Screenplay by Vincent Lawrence; additional dialogue by Mae West; based on "Single Night", an original story by Louis Bromfield.

The Night of the Iguana Screenplay by Anthony Veiller and John Huston; based on the play by Tennessee Williams.

Ninotchka Screenplay by Charles Brackett, Billy Wilder, and Walter Reisch; based on an original story by Melchior Lengyel.

Odette Screenplay by Warren Chetham-Strode.

On the Waterfront Original Screenplay by Budd Schulberg; based on "Crime on the

Waterfront", nonfiction articles by
Malcolm Johnson.

Once Upon a Honeymoon Screenplay by
Sheridan Gibney; based on an original
story by Leo McCarey.

One Flew Over the Cuckoo's Nest Screenplay by
Lawrence Hauben and Bo Goldman;
based on the novel by Ken Kesey.

Out of Africa Screenplay by Warren
Chetham-Strode.

Out of the Past Screenplay by Geoffrey Homes;
based on his novel, *Build My Gallows High*.

The Palm Beach Story Original Screenplay by
Preston Sturges.

The Paradine Case Screenplay by David O.
Selznick; adaptation by Alma Reville and
James Bridie; based on the novel by
Robert Hichens.

Pete Kelly's Blues Original Screenplay by
Richard L. Breen.

Pete 'n' Tillie Screenplay by Julius J. Epstein;
based on *Witch's Milk*, a novella by Peter
De Vries.

The Petrified Forest Screenplay by Delmer
  Daves and Charles Kenyon; based on the
  play by Robert E. Sherwood.

Peyton Place Screenplay by John Michael
  Hayes; based on the novel by Grace
  Metalious.

The Philadelphia Story Screenplay by Donald
  Ogden Stewart; based on the play by
  Philip Barry.

The Picture of Dorian Gray Screenplay by Albert
  Lewin; based on the novel by Oscar
  Wilde.

Pillow Talk Screenplay by Stanley Shapiro and
  Maurice Richlin; based on a story by
  Russell Rouse and Clarence Greene.

The Pleasure of his Company Screenplay by
  Samuel A. Taylor.

Possessed Screenplay by Syliva Richards and
  Ranald MacDougall; based on *One Man's
  Secret*, a novelette by Rita Weiman.

The President's Analyst Screenplay by Theodore
  J. Flicker.

The Prime of Miss Jean Brodie Screenplay by Jay

Presson Allen; based on her play and the novel by Muriel Spark.

The Prince and the Pauper Screenplay by Laird Doyle; based on the novel by Mark Twain.

The Private Life of Henry VIII Original Screenplay by Lajos Biro and Arthur Wimperis.

Private Lives Screenplay by Hans Kraly, Richard Schayer, and Claudine West; based on the play by Noel Coward.

The Producers Original Screenplay by Mel Brooks.

Psycho Screenplay by Joseph Stefano; based on the novel by Robert Bloch.

The Purple Heart Screenplay by Jerome Cady; based on a story by Melville Crossman.

Pygmalion Screenplay by George Bernard Shaw; adaptation by W.P. Lipscomb, Cecil Lewis, and Ian Dalrymple; based on the play by George Bernard Shaw.

The Quiet Man Screenplay by Frank S. Nugent; based on "Green Rushes", a short story by Maurice Walsh.

Quo Vadis Screenplay by John Lee Mahin, S.N. Behrman, and Sonya Levien; based on the novel by Henryk Sienkiewicz.

The Razor's Edge Screenplay by Lamar Trotti; based on the novel by W. Somerset Maugham.

Rebecca Screenplay by Robert E. Sherwood and Joan Harrison; adaptation by Philip MacDonald and Michael Hogan; based on the novel by Daphne du Maurier.

Rebel Without a Cause Screenplay by Stewart Stern; adaptation by Irving Shulman; based on an original story by Nicholas Ray.

Reflections in a Golden Eye Screenplay by Chapman Mortimer and Gladys Hill; based on the novel by Carson McCullers.

Road to Bali Screenplay by Frank Butler, Hal Kanter, and William Morrow; based on an original story by Frank Butler and Harry Tugend.

Road to Rio Original Screenplay by Edmund Beloin and Jack Rose.

The Roaring Twenties Screenplay by Richard Macaulay, Jerry Wald, and Robert

Rossen; based on a story by Mark Hellinger.

Sands of Iwo Jima Screenplay by Harry Brown and James Edward Grant; based on a story by Harry Brown.

Separate Tables Screenplay by Terence Rattigan and John Gay; based on the play by Terence Rattigan.

The Seven Year Itch Screenplay by Billy Wilder and George Axelrod; based on the play by George Axelrod.

She Done Him Wrong Screenplay by Harvey Thew and John Bright; based on *Diamond Lil*, a play by Mae West.

A Shot in the Dark Screenplay by Blake Edwards and William Peter Blatty.

The Sign of the Cross Screenplay by Waldemar Young and Sidney Buchman.

Sitting Pretty Screenplay by F. Hugh Herbert; based on the novel by Gwen Davenport.

Sleeper Screenplay by Woody Allen.

Some Like It Hot Screenplay by Billy Wilder

and I.A.L. Diamond; suggested by a story by R. Thoeren and M. Logan.

Son of Paleface Original Screenplay by Frank Tashlin, Robert L. Welch, and Joseph Quillan.

The Sound of Music Screenplay by Ernest Lehman; based on the musical play by Howard Lindsay and Russel Crouse and *The Trapp Family Singers*, a book by Maria Augusta Trapp.

Spellbound Screenplay by Ben Hecht; adaptation by Angus MacPhail; based on *The House of Dr. Edwardes*, a novel by Francis Beeding.

A Star Is Born Screenplay by Moss Hart; based on a screenplay by Dorothy Parker, Alan Campbell and Robert Carson and original story by William A. Wellman and Robert Carson.

The Sting Original Screenplay by David S. Ward.

A Streetcar Named Desire Screenplay by Tennessee Williams; adaptation by Oscar Saul; based on the play by Tennessee Williams.

Suddenly, Last Summer Screenplay by Gore Vidal and Tennessee Williams; based on the one-act play by Tennessee Williams.

Summer Holiday Screenplay by Irving Brecher and Jean Holloway; based on *Ah, Wilderness!*, a screenplay by Albert Hackett and Frances Goodrich and play by Eugene O'Neill.

Summer Wishes, Winter Dreams Original Screenplay by Stewart Stern.

Sunset Boulevard Original Screenplay by Charles Brackett, Billy Wilder, and D.M. Marshman Jr.

The Sunshine Boys Screenplay by Neil Simon; based on his play.

Sweet Bird of Youth Screenplay by Richard Brooks; based on the play by Tennessee Williams.

Take the Money and Run Original Screenplay by Woody Allen and Mickey Rose.

A Tale of Two Cities Screenplay by W.P. Lipscomb and S.N. Behrman; based on the novel by Charles Dickens.

A Taste of Honey Screenplay by Shelagh

Delaney and Tony Richardson; based on the play by Shelagh Delaney.

The Teahouse of the August Moon Screenplay by John Patrick; based on his play and the book by Vern J. Sneider.

They Drive By Night Screenplay by Jerry Wald and Richard Macaulay; based on *Long Haul,* a novel by A.I. Bezzerides.

They Knew What They Wanted Screenplay by Robert Ardrey; based on the play by Sidney Howard.

The Thin Man Screenplay by Albert Hackett and Frances Goodrich; based on the novel by Dashiell Hammett.

The Third Man Original Screenplay by Graham Greene.

A Thousand Clowns Screenplay by Herb Gardner; based on his play.

Tom Jones Screenplay by John Osborne; based on the novel by Henry Fielding.

Torrid Zone Original Screenplay by Richard Macaulay and Jerry Wald.

True Grit Screenplay by Marguerite Roberts; based on the novel by Charles Portis.

An Unmarried Woman Original Screenplay by Paul Mazursky.

Watch on the Rhine Screenplay by Dashiell Hammett; additional scenes and dialogue by Lillian Hellman; based on her play.

We're No Angels Screenplay by Ranald MacDougall; based on *La Cuisine des Anges*, a play by Albert Husson, and *My Three Angels*, a Broadway adaptation by Bella Spewack and Samuel Spewack.

What's Up, Doc? Screenplay by Buck Henry, David Newman and Robert Benton; based on a story by Peter Bogdanovich.

Who's Afraid of Virginia Woolf? Screenplay by Ernest Lehman; based on the play by Edward Albee.

Woman of the Year Original Screenplay by Ring Lardner Jr. and Michael Kanin.

The Women Screenplay by Anita Loos and Jane Murfin; based on the play by Clare Boothe.

Wuthering Heights Screenplay by Ben Hecht

and Charles MacArthur; based on the novel by Emily Brontë.

Zorba the Greek Screenplay by Michael Cacoyannis; based on the novel by Nikos Kazantzakis.